GW00938992

*T*o ..Mum..............

*F*rom ..Lynn,. David........
David + Katie

"*Romance fails us - and so do friendships - but the relationship of - Mother and Child - remains indelible and indestructible - the strongest bond upon this earth.*"

THEODOR REIK,
from "Of Love and Lust"

"*Nobody can have the soul of me.*
My mother has had it, and nobody can
have it again. Nobody can come into my
very self again, and breathe me in
like an atmosphere."

D.H. LAWRENCE (1885-1930)

Hundreds of stars in the pretty sky,
Hundreds of shells on the shore together,
Hundreds of birds that go singing by,
Hundreds of birds in the sunny weather,
Hundreds of dewdrops to greet the dawn,
Hundreds of bees in the purple clover,
Hundreds of butterflies on the lawn,
But only one mother the wide world over.

GEORGE COOPER

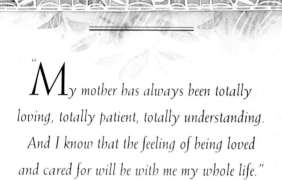

"My mother has always been totally loving, totally patient, totally understanding. And I know that the feeling of being loved and cared for will be with me my whole life."

HELEN THOMSON, b.1943

"A mother is she who can take the place of all others but whose place no one else can take."

CARDINAL MERMILLOD

"*Everybody knows that a good mother gives her children a feeling of trust and stability. She is the one they can count on for the things that matter most of all. She is their food and their bed and their extra blanket when it grows cold in the night; she is their warmth and health and their shelter; she is the one they want to be near when they cry. She is the only person in the whole world or in a whole lifetime who can be these things to her children. There is no substitute for her. Somehow even her clothes feel different to her children's hands from anybody else's clothes. Only to touch her skirt or her sleeve makes a troubled child feel better.*"

KATHARINE BUTLER HATHAWAY

"Mother is food; she is love;
she is warmth; she is earth.
To be loved by her means
to be alive,
to be rooted,
to be at home."

ERICH FROMM (1900-1980)

"*The most powerful ties are the ones to the people who gave birth to us...it hardly seems to matter how many years have passed, how many betrayals there may have been, how much misery in the family; we remain connected, even against our wills.*"

ANTHONY BRANDT

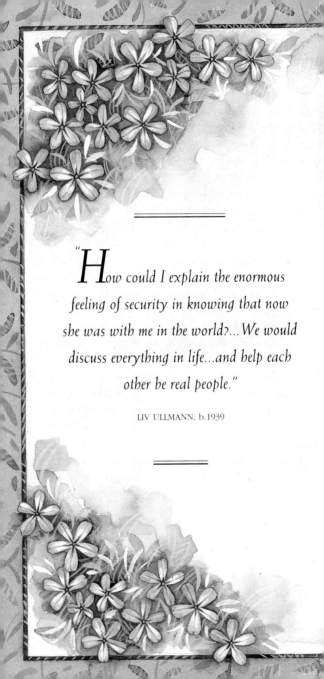

"*How* could I explain the enormous feeling of security in knowing that now she was with me in the world?...We would discuss everything in life...and help each other be real people."

LIV ULLMANN, b.1939

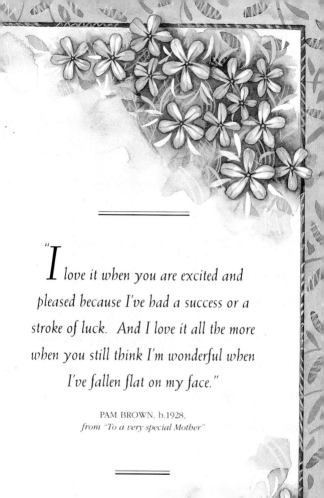

"*I* love it when you are excited and pleased because I've had a success or a stroke of luck. And I love it all the more when you still think I'm wonderful when I've fallen flat on my face."

PAM BROWN, b.1928,
from "To a very special Mother"

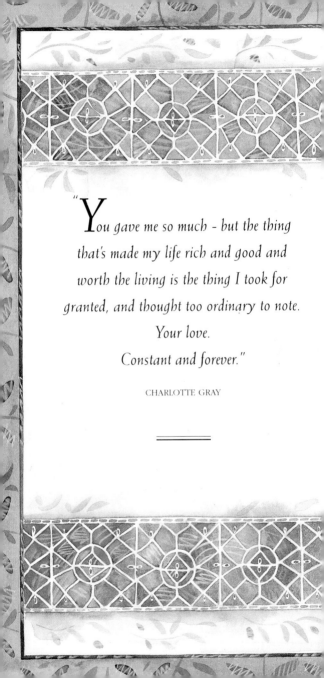

"*You gave me so much - but the thing that's made my life rich and good and worth the living is the thing I took for granted, and thought too ordinary to note. Your love. Constant and forever.*"

CHARLOTTE GRAY

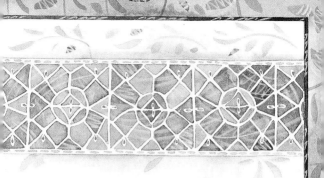

To her whose heart is my
heart's quiet home,
To my first Love,
my Mother on whose knee
I learnt love-lore that is not troublesome:
Whose service is my special dignity
And she my lodestar while I go and come.

CHRISTINA ROSSETTI (1830-1894)

"*There never was a woman like her. She was gentle as a dove and brave as a lioness.... The memory of my mother and her teachings were after all the only capital I had to start life with, and on that capital I have made my way.*"

ANDREW JACKSON

"My mother was the making of me.
She was so true and so sure of me, I felt
that I had someone to live for - someone I
must not disappoint. The memory of my
mother will always be a blessing to me."

THOMAS A. EDISON (1847-1931)

"My mother taught me to walk proud
and tall 'as if the world was mine.'"

SOPHIA LOREN, b.1934

"*When* mamma smiled, beautiful as her face was, it grew incomparably more lovely, and everything around seemed brighter.
If in life's sad moments I could but have had a glimpse of that smile I should not have known what sorrow is."

COUNT LEO NIKOLAIEVICH TOLSTOY (1828-1910)

"I think my life began with waking up and loving my mother's face."

GEORGE ELIOT (MARY ANN EVANS) (1819-1880)

Gentle hands that never weary of toiling in love's vineyard sweet, eyes that seem forever cheery when our eyes they chance to meet. Tender, patient, brave, devoted - this is always mother's way....

PAUL C. BROWNLOW

"A mother is the truest friend we have, when trials, heavy and sudden, fall upon us; when adversity takes the place of prosperity; when friends who rejoice with us in our sunshine, desert us when troubles thicken around us, still will she cling to us, and endeavor by her kind precepts and counsels to dissipate the clouds of darkness, and cause peace to return to our hearts."

WASHINGTON IRVING (1783-1859)

"*Who is it that loves me and will love me forever with an affection which no chance, no misery, no crime of mine can do away? It is you, my mother.*"

THOMAS CARLYLE (1795-1881)

"*That dear octopus from whose tentacles we never quite escape, nor in our innermost hearts never quite wish to.*"

DODIE SMITH (1896-1990)

"*In after life you may have friends fond, dear friends, but never will you have again the inexpressible love and gentleness lavished upon you which none but a Mother bestows.*"

THOMAS BABINGTON MACAULAY (1800-1859)

"You mothers have a habit of blaming yourself for everything that goes wrong. You were so determined to get it right - to bring us up perfectly. You forget. There's never a rehearsal. For every child is totally unlike the others.

Of course you made mistakes. But I don't want a perfect mother. I want one who is human and can understand - and lets me make my own catastrophes. You haven't feet of clay, just ordinary human feet - subject to callouses and fallen arches.

I love you exactly as you are."

PAM BROWN, b.1928

"My mother wanted me to be her wings, to fly as she never quite had the courage to do. I love her for that. I love the fact that she wanted to give birth to her own wings."

ERICA JONG, b.1942

"*Thanks for never thinking me perfect.*
That way I was allowed to make mistakes.
And that way I was allowed to grow."

CLARA ORTEGA

"*My mother raised me,*
and then freed me."

MAYA ANGELOU, b.1928

———

"*If a thing was worth seeing, or hearing or smelling or touching or testing - you would get me there - come hell or high water, come mud, snow, rain or lack of cash in hand.*

Thank you for a life filled with memories to see me through."

PAM BROWN, b.1928

———